BITTER-SWEET

BITTER-SWEET

ANDREW WATERMAN

Shoestring Press

Printed by imprintdigital
Upton Pyne, Exeter
www.digital.imprint.co.uk

Typesetting and cover design by narrator
www.narrator.me.uk
info@narrator.me.uk
033 022 300 39

Published by Shoestring Press
19 Devonshire Avenue, Beeston, Nottingham, NG9 1BS
(0115) 925 1827
www.shoestringpress.co.uk

First published 2017
© Copyright: Andrew Waterman

ISBN 978-1-910323-77-9

ALSO BY ANDREW WATERMAN

Living Room (Marvell Press)
From the Other Country (Carcanet Press)
Over the Wall (Carcanet Press)
Out for the Elements (Carcanet Press)
Selected Poems (Carcanet Press)
In the Planetarium (Carcanet Press)
The End of the Pier Show (Carcanet Press)
Collected Poems 1959–1999 (Carcanet Press)
The Captain's Swallow (Carcanet Press)
By the River Wensum (Shoestring Press)

(Editor) *The Poetry of Chess* (Anvil Press)

For Veronica

PREFACE

In the very last poem of this short sequence Andrew Waterman states: "In me no rich experience is completed / unless it's shared: these places, / music, my sense of wonder. Jokes." Waterman has been sharing his rich experience with readers for over forty years now and these poems show the same unfailing sense of wonder, and the same power to transmit it to the reader. His feeling for place and time, which has always been one of his greatest gifts, is fully on display here, as he takes us from Norwich to Sicily and Tuscany over a period of three years. Although the sequence contains only seven poems, he manages to give us a full and touching picture of a developing relationship, thanks to his skill at capturing significant moments against a background of the changing seasons in England and Italy. In an earlier poem, "By the River Wensum", Waterman said that such moments are "how lives define themselves"; he doesn't merely pinpoint these moments, but succeeds in conveying the full intensity of the experience to the reader. And the jokes are there too, in particular in the several delightful pictures of animals, from the squirrel that opens and closes the sequence to the swans with "necks like question-marks uncoiling", to the "small dog Dior", who lords it over a park in Taormina. Waterman's poetic vision and his capacity for wonder remain as lucid as ever.

Gregory Darling
Professor of English at the University of Venice

1   NOVEMBER, NORWICH

You watch the squirrel looking back at you
from its low bough among trees clustering
the dips and slopes of Mousehold Heath,
carpeting them with leaves we scrunch through.

You must cut short this visit.
Flying from Sicily you had just learnt
of your mother's illness: cancer of the colon.
They operate, in Romania, today.

You must go there. Here all is peaceful,
no breeze, birds trill, a couple walk their dog,
you ask its name, then stoop to hug it.
You lean against a rough-barked trunk, then hug it.

2   AT RIVER GREEN

Swans' necks like question-marks uncoiling
dart chest-high at you grabbing the bread
you've brought, on this stretch of grass
by the drift of the Yare. Behind us shops, a church.

The ducks, your favourites,
are crowded out, can't get a morsel, when
you lob a chunk out over the water
gulls swoop to snatch it in mid-air.

I've heard a single blow from a swan's wing
can break an arm. 'Steer clear of them,' they say.
The bread's all gone, yet still they pester you,
and still you are smiling.

3 ELY

The 'Ship of the Fens': its lantern tower
soars above flatlands and this small city
perched up from them. Inside,
lofty spaciousness, niches with delicate carvings.

And the Stained-Glass Museum:
eye to eye we stare at saints and sinners,
martyrs and monsters, vividly lit.

We leave the Cathedral: outside, a kempt Green,
Georgian architecture and older stuff,
the Bishop's Palace, Cromwell's house.
Lunch in a pub, then we stroll to the river
and saunter along its towpath.

Back down the meadow to the station
there is a tree, its foliage so intensely
russet it looks like petals;
a horse trots to a gate to nuzzle your hand.

You love all this. I love the way you love it.

'Yes,' you reply, looking out from our train,
at low fertile fields, 'this looks like
where I grew up.' On a branch of the eastern Danube.

You go there tomorrow to your ill mother.

4   PHONE CALL

'*Da, eu sunt Andrew,*' I say, and '*Buna seara!*'
Which about exhausts my knowledge of the language.
You've put your mother on the phone to me
 from the hospital. I don't know what she's saying.
'I wish you good health!' I say uselessly.
'*Multumesc,*' she says. I know that's 'Thank you.'

You've told me that although the operation
went well, the evil cells have spread.

Your voice again. Will I go,
 you ask me, to your favourite church in Norwich,
St Peter Mancroft poised over the market,
 and sit and sit and think for a while?'

Years ago, in December darkness
 chancing past its floodlit shapeliness
we halted, rapt, stunned by sudden whirl
 of luminous snowflakes dancing.

5   DIOR

I don't know how he knows it, but he knows it:
your footstep on the steps up from the Corso
among others who pass up or down.
From wherever he is in your apartment
he scampers to the door, and as your key
scrapes in the latch, he levitates,
rotates through 360 degrees and lands tail wagging.

Your small dog Dior, a black blob of nose,
soft pointy ears. As always when I'm here
I take him for enormous walks
along the Corso, up steps to the market
or down steps to the Public Gardens
where he loves sniffing shrubs and tree-trunks.
Walking a dog one gets to talk with people;
some think I live here, ask me for directions.

Best is when we go together with him,
when your work allows, to '*il suo parco*':
the gardens of Hotel Excelsior Palace
where you've permission to walk him.
Here he can roam off-lead.
He strolls up past the swimming-pool, then turns
and hurtles down, a golden streak,
and leaps up at us panting for caresses.
He has his favourite vantage-points:
one can look up to the left to Taormina's
ancient Greek theatre or up to the right
and Etna's great hulk fuming.
Dior knows nothing of such things
nor of the hotel. This is his park.
He gazes out through railings on a brink
looking for butterflies, or far down, ears twitching,
when a train trundles tinily along the coast.

Next week when I'm back home in England you
fly again to Romania to visit
your mother in hospital. On your return
his joy will hit the roof.

6   MISSED

The doctors promised that they'd contact you
to let you know when the end was near.

It happened too swiftly. When the call came
your mother had already died.

All you reached was the funeral.
'Now I am at the grave,' you tell me,

'On the flight I felt that she was with me,
now I'm here all seems senseless.'

Gripping my phone, I stare at Spring,
gold sprawls of daffodils along the river.

'I wish,' you say, 'I could have got here in time
to share some memories with her. And jokes.'

7   IN FLORENCE

'*La nostra vacanza meravigliosa.*'
You've flown from Sicily and I from London,
Tuscany being half-way between.
In Pisa I took the photo so many take,
you posed arms stretched to prop the Leaning Tower;
in Lucca we walked the tree-lined walls
strewn with fallen leaves.

None of Florence's sumptuous stuff was built
when Dante walked here, though they'd started
on the Palazzo Vecchio. We admire
the pillars in its inner courtyard.
Strolling to our hotel you say,
'I so often think of Beeston Hill.
In one direction the whole sky was sunset,
in the other the brilliant full moon.'

'*Anch'io,*' I say. Me too.
I'm looking up at Brunelleschi's dome
magically floated above the rooftops.
'It lives in me too.' We'd climbed the hill,
300-and-something feet, not bad for Norfolk,
and from the top there it was:
the western sky a flood of red and gold,
the other way a full moon off the cliff-edge.
We swung from one to the other and then back
and swivelled back again, thrilling.

In me no rich experience is completed
unless it's shared: these places,
music, my sense of wonder. Jokes.

And when, three years ago, I watched
you watch a squirrel looking back at you
from its low bough on Mousehold Heath.